Paleo

Lose The Wheat
Lose The Weight

by Beth Gabriel

Published in United States by:

Beth Gabriel

© Copyright 2014 – Beth Gabriel

ISBN-13: 978-1502789020
ISBN-10: 1502789027

ALL RIGHTS RESERVED. No part of this publication may be reproduced or transmitted in any form whatsoever, electronic, or mechanical, including photocopying, recording, or by any informational storage or retrieval system without express written, dated and signed permission from the author.

Download your FREE printable PDF of the meal plans and shopping lists here: http://PaleoRecipesWeightLoss.com/bonus

Table of Contents

Welcome To A New Leaner You 7
   The Who, What and Why of Paleo 8

Paleo Meal Plans 13
   Meal Plan #1 13
   Meal Plan #2 16
   Meal Plan #3 18

Paleo Recipes 21
Appetizers 21
   Shrimp Cocktail With Zing 21
   Sesame Crisp Crackers 23
   Hummus With A Twist 25
   Sweet Potato Basil Bruschetta 26
   Fried Avocado, Sweet & Sour Sauce 28
   Brussels Sprouts Prosciutto Kabobs 30
   Toasted Roasted Turnips 32
   Summer Fresh Fruit Kebobs 34
   Cumin Sweet Potato Fries 36
   Lamb Stuffed Grape Leaves 38

Main Dish Recipes 41

Orange Grilled Chicken 41
　　Thyme Salmon with Leek Coulis Sauce 45
　　Asian Coconut Cauli-Rice Lettuce Wraps 47
　　Butternut Squash Harvest Lasagna 50
　　Lemon Garlic Crockpot Chicken 52
　　Poblano Chorizo Stuffed Peppers 54
　　Sweet Potato Zucchini Frittata 55
　　Honey Glazed Garlic Chicken Wings 57
　　Zesty Roasted Leg of Lamb 59

Side Dish Recipes 61
　　Spicy Smashed Sweet Potatoes 62
　　Fried Rice Cauliflower Style 65
　　Orange and Ginger Glazed Carrots 67
　　Mexican Rice Cauliflower Inspired 69
　　Sesame Noodles 71
　　Almond Yorkshire Pudding 73
　　Zucchini Noodles With Creamy Avocado 75
　　Italian Breaded Eggplant 77
　　Sweet Potato Rolls 79
　　Roasted Toasted Garlic Mushrooms 81

Soup Recipes 83
　　Carrot Orange Ginger Soup 83
　　Chicken Stock From Scratch 86
　　Mushroom Kale Chicken Soup 88
　　Chicken Zucchini Noodle Soup 90

Salad Recipes 91
　　Pomegranate Arugula Salad 91
　　Kale Grapefruit Salad 93
　　Orange Cherry Mesclun Salad 94

Dessert Recipes 95
    Banoffee Cashew Cheesecake 95
    Apple Pie Parfaits 100
    Strawberry Leather 103
    Coconut Butter Stuffed Dates........................... 104
    Fruit Dip 105

Snack Recipes... 107
    Coconut Chicken Nuggets BBQ Sauce 107
    Egg Muffins 111
    Chicken-And-Egg-Stuffed Tomatoes 113
    Guacamole Eggs 114
    Lime Chicken Wings 115
    Yummy Fish Sticks 117
    Fruit Nutty Energy Bars................................... 119
    Blueberry Balls 121
    Prosciutto Chips.. 122
    Herb Crackers... 123

Thank You! 125
Book Recommendations................................... 127

Welcome To A New Leaner You

The Paleo diet is not a typical "diet" at all. It's the return to the essential food that our ancestors ate. The whole idea of the Paleo lifestyle is that if a caveman didn't eat it, neither should you. Don't be fooled, the Paleo diet contains an abundance of great tasting food. You won't be left feeling like you're missing out on anything.

In the spirit of eating great tasting, healthy meals that are easy to prepare, we have put together a book of great tasting recipes. Each recipe is designed to make meals stress-free and fun when you gather with friends and family around your dinner table.

Creating a complete Paleo meal from start to finish can seem a bit overwhelming but rest easy, we've given you 3 full meal plans complete with shopping lists. These meal plans contain everything from appetizers to dessert, so you can't go wrong.

The Who, What and Why of Paleo

On The Origins...

Back in the B.C. ages, people were hunting and gathering machines. They lived running around and eating what they found for half a million years. Compared to that, our couple of thousands of years as an agricultural society dims in importance. Over that tremendous period of earlier time, our bodies were agile and capable of working with little fuel. Nowadays, we eat much more than we actual need, because we are still designed as we were 20 thousand years ago. We are literally overstuffing ourselves and we don't even feel it. We're clustering our bodies, becoming increasingly tired, depressed and out of shape.

In this age when you can eat anything and everything, we suggest you step back and understand exactly what you are eating. Look closely and you will see. We're eating tons of bread, tons of sugar, tons of fat. When you put it all together, no wonder your body is fighting against you.

Here's How Paleo Works...

You simply take out all of the processed food that early man never ate. Yes, all of it. Fibers, glucoses and lipids. Dairy products, chemicals, processed food. You clean your body of all the unnecessary fuel that is blocking it and storing itself on your hips and heart as fat. Most modern diseases can be prevented by simply eating healthily, so why complicate your life?

Paleo is all about natural food. You eliminate the overly-processed supermarket meals and gain your energy from the sun and wind and freedom. Sounds romantic? It is. If the fruits you eat are from ecological orchards, if your meat hasn't been treated with a million chemicals, if you can bite from an apple and actually feel its taste, then nature is literally feeding you. I'll start with what to avoid, so you can be joyful later.

What To Avoid

Sugar – this is an obvious one, but the most necessary one. Sweets give you nothing. You think they give you energy? Think again. It takes twice as much to process a chocolate bar than it takes to eat a full plate of vegetables, with some chicken on the side. My favorite motivation to give up sweets was this: in order to get rid of all the calories in just two M&M candies (not bags, candies), you would have to run around a football field. What's easier for you? Running a quarter mile or letting sugar go?

Grains – this is bread, basically. While most people just talk about the fattening part, the health part is even more dramatic. Grains are made of carbs and cavemen didn't eat it for a reason, even if they couldn't understand it back then. Carbs come into our body and turn themselves into glucose, which would be ok, if you were still running over hills every minute of every day. All that glucose is stored as fat, because it's not used. Not only that, but grains also contain lectin. Lectin is toxic. Toxic things shouldn't get into your body. Lectin affects the intestines and slowly causes damage around there. Bread is hard to give up on, but it's the utter most important part of Paleo. Always remember: if a caveman didn't eat it, neither should you.

Dairy products – this one is slightly easier, as a lot of people have lactose intolerance and don't drink milk anyway. But for the rest of us, cereal-lovers, giving up on our morning cup can be hard. However, let's think it like this. Humans are the only mammals that continue to drink milk after infancy. Nobody else does that, as our stomachs are not built to deal with the processing of lactose, which is a pretty tough job, thus stealing your energy.

Ok, you made it. Now, if you're hungry, let's see what exactly you can eat.

What To Eat

- Meat – non-processed, of course. The more organic, the better.
- Fish – now you have an excuse to go fishing
- Birds
- Eggs
- Natural oils – coconut oil, olive oil, etc.
- Good carbs – the good cop is here and you'll find it in vegetables and sweet potatoes
- Fruits
- Vegetables
- Seeds
- Nuts
- Honey

Lose The Wheat, Lose The Weight

The best news? The Paleo diet is the best diet for losing weight, because it relies on you're not getting hungry. All of this food is nourishing and one plate of it will keep you satisfied for hours, while potato chips will demand a new bag every other minute.

The best idea is to eat a bit of everything at each meal, thus having a balanced meal. You cannot possibly overeat when you're on Paleo (that sounds a bit like we're talking medicine, but I guess it fits). Feel like eating?

Have an apple, have a bunch. Still hungry? Have some nuts. Need more? Eat a carrot. See? Tons of food and none on the hips. Everything you eat is digested fast and you will feel that extra boost as the day goes by.

So over the next 70+ pages, we shall delve deep into all the yummy things you can cook, that will clean your body of unwanted fat and give you energy, joy and a healthy excuse to go to the hills every now and then. Maybe you'll discover running is really fun after all. Maybe you'll pick up a camera and film the birds at dawn. Maybe you'll meet the love of your life on a trip on the beach. Energy has its perks.

Welcome to the Paleo Lifestyle!

Paleo Meal Plans

Meal Plan #1

- **Appetizer** : Hummus With A Twist
- **Main Dish** : Honey Glazed Garlic Chicken Wings
- **Side Dish** : Fried Rice Cauliflower Style
- **Salad** : Cherry Orange Mesclun Salad
- **Dessert** : Fruit Dip

Shopping List

Meat
3 Pounds Chicken Wings

Vegetables
4 Cups Peeled & Chopped Raw Zucchini
4 Cloves of Garlic - Peeled
2 Tbsp. Garlic – Chopped
1 Head of Cauliflower
4 Carrots - Peeled and Chopped
1 Small Onion - Chopped
1 Cup Green Peas
4 Cups Mesclun Greens (or similar mixed, young greens)

Fruit
3/4 Cup Fresh Lemon Juice
2 Ripe Bananas
3 Oranges
1 Cup Cherries

Seasonings, Oils & Miscellaneous
3/4 Cups Tahini (Sesame Paste)
1/4 Cup Sesame Seeds
6 Tablespoons Olive Oil
2 Teaspoons Garlic Powder

2 Teaspoons Kosher Salt (Or To Taste)
1 Tablespoon Ground Cumin
1/3 Cup Honey
1/4 Cup Water
8 Tablespoons Coconut Aminos
2 Tablespoons Apple Cider Vinegar
3/4 Teaspoon Ground Ginger
1/2 Teaspoon Sesame Oil
1/2 Teaspoon Fish Sauce
1 Cup Coconut Milk
1 Teaspoon Vanilla
2 Teaspoons Coconut Flour
1 1/2 Tablespoons Unsweetened Cocoa Powder (Optional)
2 Tablespoons Balsamic Vinegar

Dairy & Refriderated Items
4 Tablespoons Lard
4 Eggs

Meal Plan #2

- **Appetizer** : Toasted Brussels Sprouts Shish Kabobs
- **Main Dish** : Zesty Roasted Leg of Lamb
- **Side Dish** : Spicy Smashed Sweet Potatoes
- **Dessert** : Banoffee Cashew Cheesecake

Shopping List

Meat
1/4 Pound Prosciutto - Thinly Sliced
4-5 Pound Leg of Lamb (Boneless Or Bone In)

Vegetables
1 Pound Small Brussels Sprouts
2 Medium Sized Sweet Potatoes

Fruit & Nuts
Zest of 2 Lemons – about 4 Tablespoons
2 Cups Raw Cashews
3 Medium Sized Ripe Bananas

Seasonings, Oils & Miscellaneous
2 Tablespoons Extra-Virgin Olive Oil
1/4 Cup Fresh Oregano
5-6 Cloves Fresh Garlic
Salt
1/2 Teaspoon Cracked Pepper
1/2 Teaspoon Chili Powder
1/2 Teaspoon Cumin
1/2 Teaspoon Garlic Powder
1/2 Teaspoon Onion Powder
1/2 Teaspoon Paprika
Ground Black Pepper
1 Cup Almond Flour
1 Cup Ghee
7/8 Cup Raw Honey
2 Teaspoons Vanilla Extract
Dash Cacao Powder
2 Cans (13/14 Oz.) Full Fat Coconut Milk

Meal Plan #3

- **Appetizer** : Fried Avocado With Sweet & Sour
- **Main Dish** : Chicken Zucchini Noodle Soup
- **Side Dish** : Orange And Ginger Glazed Carrots
- **Salad** : Kale Grapefruit Salad
- **Dessert** : Apple Pie Parfaits

Shopping List

Meat
1 Quart Chicken Stock (or use our recipe in the 'Soup' section of this book)

Vegetables
1 Rib Celery – Diced
5 Celery Tops
1 Small Zucchini
1 Onion
1 1/2 Pounds Carrots
1 Bunch Kale

Fruit
2 Avocados
1 Orange
1 Lime
1 Grapefruit
5 Large Apples

Seasonings, Oils & Miscellaneous
10 Cloves Garlic
1/4 Cup Parsley
10 Sprigs Fresh Thyme
2 Bay Leaves
1/3 Cup Coconut Flour
1 Teaspoon Garlic Powder
Coconut Oil for Frying
1 Tablespoon Apple Cider Vinegar

Water
1/2 Teaspoon Ground Ginger
Ground Black Pepper
1/2 Cup Ghee
3 Tablespoons Ghee
1 Cup Raw Honey
1/2 Teaspoon Ground Cinnamon
1 Teaspoon Vanilla Extract
1 Teaspoon Arrowroot Powder
3/4 Cup Blanched Almond Flour
1 Can (13/14 Oz.) Full Fat Coconut Milk
1 Tablespoon Vanilla Extract
1 Tablespoon Olive Oil
Celtic Sea Salt
1 Teaspoon Balsamic Vinegar

Dairy & Refriderated Items

2 Eggs
Splash of Milk (Dairy, Coconut, Almond) - optional
2 Tablespoons Grated Parmesan Cheese - optional
1 Tablespoon Lard

Paleo Recipes

Appetizers

Shrimp Cocktail With Zing

For hot summer evenings, this is the best for a leisurely first course.

Ingredients
1 1/2 Pounds Pre-Cooked Shrimp, deveined & shell removed

Cocktail Sauce

8 Oz. Can Tomato Sauce
1 Tablespoon Prepared Yellow Mustard
1 Tablespoon Horseradish
1/2 Teaspoon Garlic Powder
3 Teaspoons Freshly Squeezed Lemon Juice
1/2 Teaspoon Raw Honey
Sea Salt
Ground Pepper
Lemon Slices

Directions

1. Combine all sauce ingredients in a bowl and stir. Let the sauce chill in the refrigerator for 1-2 hours.
2. Set the cocktail sauce in a small bowl over a larger bowl filled with crushed ice to keep chilled. Around the rim, hang the shrimp and lemon slices.
3. Relax and enjoy!

Sesame Crisp Crackers

We all love crackers and since grains are out of bounds for Paleo, these crisps will clear away your cravings and offer you a bunch of fulfilling crackers, with a brilliant taste. The raisins will give them all the sweetness they need and they're low on fat, too.

Ingredients
1/2 Cup Dates
1/2 Cup Raisins
1/2 Cup Sliced Almonds
1/4 Cup Each Sunflower Seeds, Pepitas, Sesame Seeds
1/4 Cup Each Almond Flour, Flaxseed Meal.
1/2 Teaspoon Sea Salt
2 Tablespoons Water

Directions
1. Pulse dates and raisins together in food processor.
2. Grind evenly.
3. Add in all the seeds, almonds, salt, flour, meal and the water.
4. Blend together well until it is sticking together.

5. Roll the dough between two parchment papers until they get really thin (approximately 1/8 inch thickness).
6. Do this in 2 or 3 batches.
7. Bake for 30 minutes, until lightly browned, nice and crispy.
8. Use a sharp knife to cut them into equal size chips. Let cool.
9. Great when served with the <u>Hummus recipe</u> listed below

Hummus With A Twist

One of the tastiest Turkish appetizers is hummus. This recipe replaces the typical Garbanzo beans with Zucchini. Natural, creamy and with great nutritional value, this paste can be eaten with Sesame crisp crackers or Herb rolls, both available in this book. Or you can eat it like custard. It's still delicious.

Ingredients
4 Cups Raw Zucchini - Peeled & Chopped
3/4 Cup Tahini (Sesame Paste)
1/2 Cup Fresh Lemon Juice
1/4 Cup Olive Oil
4 Cloves Garlic - Peeled
2 Teaspoons Kosher Salt (or to taste)
1 Tablespoon Ground Cumin

Directions
1. Add all the ingredients in a blender and puree until thick and smooth.
2. Pour into a bowl and adorn with paprika, parsley and some olive oil if desired.
3. Serve with <u>Sesame Crisps Crackers</u> , <u>Herb Crackers</u> or <u>Paleo Rolls</u>, all recipes available in this book.

Sweet Potato Basil Bruschetta

Bruschettas are Italian born. Whether you love them with tomatoes, onions or, in our case, sweet potatoes, it's the olive oil that gives it the classical taste. Feel free to make as many as you like and to eat as many as your conscience allows you.

Ingredients
1 Sweet Potato
Oil Of Choice (Coconut, Olive Oil or Ghee)
Vinaigrette - 3 Parts Olive Oil To 1 Part Red Wine Vinegar, Minced Garlic Clove, Salt, Pepper)
2-3 Tomatoes - Chopped Fine
Black Olives - Chopped
Fresh Basil- Chopped
Fresh Parmesan (Optional)

Directions
1. Peel the sweet potato and slice it length-wise, in pieces about 1/4" thick
2. Brown the slices in a frying pan over medium heat, in the oil.

3. Cook it for 10 minutes, until it is golden brown.
4. Mix basil, tomatoes and olives in the vinaigrette to coat them.
5. Lay the potatoes out on a baking sheet and cover with the tomato mixture.
6. Optional - add a touch of parmesan, for that extra Italian taste.
7. Place in a pre-heated 350°F oven for 10 minutes to warm. Or eat them cold, they're still delicious.

Fried Avocado, Sweet & Sour Sauce

Whenever people gather for football matches or a casual get together, it's only natural to serve something crunchy like chips. However, here you have a far less fattening alternative, with a real taste.

Ingredients
2 Avocados
2 Eggs
Splash Of Milk (Dairy, Coconut, Almond.)
1/3 Cup Coconut Flour
2 Tablespoons Grated Parmesan Cheese (or use Almond Flour to replace the dairy)
1 Teaspoon Garlic Powder
Salt and Pepper
Coconut Oil for Frying

Sweeet & Sour Dipping Sauce
2 Tablespoons All Natural Dijon Mustard
1 1/2 Tablespoons Balsamic Vinegar
1 Tablespoon All Natural Mayonnaise
1 Teaspoon Pure Raw Honey
1/2 Teaspoon Garlic - Minced

Directions
1. Cut avocados in half lengthwise, remove the pit. Make 3 horizontal slices per half.
2. Peel the skin and discard.
3. In a bowl, whisk the eggs and milk. In a separate bowl, combine the coconut flour, garlic powder, grated parmesan, salt and pepper.
4. Coat the avocado with the coconut mixture, then dip it in the egg mixture and then back again into the coconut flour mixture
5. Pour a few tablespoons of the oil into a skillet over medium heat.
6. Fry the avocado, until it becomes golden. It fries really quickly, so pay close attention.
7. Serve with the dipping sauce.

Dipping Sauce
1. Mix all dipping sauce ingredients together until well combined.
2. Serve with Fried Avocados.

Brussels Sprouts Prosciutto Kabobs

The Italians to the rescue again. Prosciutto gives you the addictive pizza-like flavor but Paleo style to give you all the nutrition without the grains and fat. Brilliant isn't it?

Ingredients
1 Pound Small Brussels Sprouts - rinsed with water to remove any dirt
2 Tablespoons Extra-Virgin Olive Oil
1/4 Pound Prosciutto - Thinly Sliced
1 Pinch Coarse Salt and Freshly Ground Pepper

Directions
1. Preheat oven to 400°F.
2. Slice Brussels sprouts in half lengthwise, leaving the ends.
3. Put the sprouts on a baking sheet with the oil and salt and pepper.
4. Bake for 40 minutes, but start checking after 25 minutes.
5. Toss them around in oil on sheet.
6. Cut the prosciutto in small bits.

7. Sauté it for about 5 minutes, until it becomes nice and crispy.
8. Let the sprouts cool, so you can handle them.
9. Slide half a sprout on a toothpick, follow with 3 slices of ham, then add another sprout half on the end.
10. Repeat.

Toasted Roasted Turnips

An old friend of my dad's showed me this and I've got to say, it's the best replacement to potatoes I have ever tasted. Fried, they're even better, they taste exactly like French Fries. Just cut the turnip in very thin slices, salt them and fry them really quick in a pan. Serve this to unknowing guests and watch their surprised faces when you tell them "Yeah, they really aren't potatoes". One more win for the Paleo side.

Ingredients
2 Pounds Turnips - Peeled (peel a layer past the skin)
2 Tablespoons Ghee - Melted (or other fat)
Kosher Salt
Freshly Ground Pepper

Directions
1. Cut the turnips into 1" cubes.
2. Preheat oven to 425°F
3. Toss the cut turnip cubes with salt, pepper and melted ghee.

4. On a baking tray, leave the turnips in the oven for 20-25 minutes, flipping them halfway through.
5. Bake until they're brown and tender.
6. Serve immediately, hot and fresh.

Summer Fresh Fruit Kebobs

We are surrounded by eye-candy. Everywhere you turn your head, on the street, in public places, on TV, there is always that one little beautiful thing, whether it's eatable or not, that catches your attention and says "Hold up, I've got something to tell". The same psychological principle applies to food. The more color, the better, as each color will bring a different category of vitamins. Enjoy these fresh fruit kebobs on summer evenings, with a strawberry cocktail next to you.

Ingredients & Directions
1. Buy wooden grill sticks.
2. Choose a different fruit for each color.
    - RED - Watermelon, Strawberries, Red grapes, Cherries or Raspberries
    - ORANGE - Cantaloupe, Oranges or Mangos
    - YELLOW - Pineapple or Bananas
    - GREEN - Kiwis or Green Grapes
    - BLUE/PURPLE - Purple grapes, Blackberries or Blueberries

3. Thread them on a stick, alternating colors as you go.
4. Repeat.

Cumin Sweet Potato Fries

Forget about French fries. You've got great taste with half the fate. This will help you remember how potatoes should actually taste like. Goes great with chicken or steak on the side.

Ingredients
2 Sweet Potatoes
2 Tablespoons Olive Oil
1 Teaspoon Kosher Salt
1/2 Teaspoon Freshly Ground Black Pepper
1/2 Teaspoon Ground Cumin
1/4 Teaspoon Chili Powder

Directions
1. Preheat the oven to 375°F
2. Peel the potatoes and cut each into 8 pieces.
3. Add the rest of the ingredients, making sure they get really well covered (you can use your hands for this, it makes it easier).
4. Place potatoes on a large baking tray. To ensure an even baking, lay the potatoes on their sides.
5. Bake for 20 minutes, then rotate the pan and

flip potatoes over.
6. Bake for an additional 25 extra minutes, until the potatoes are browned and soft.
7. Sprinkle with salt. Enjoy!

Lamb Stuffed Grape Leaves

Another sweet and delicious recipe, with East-European influences, are stuffed grape leaves. You can use beef or chicken instead of lamb, but for that true Turkish flavor, lamb is the best. This is a hybrid, so feel free to experiment with ingredients, for your own perfect taste.

Ingredients
1 8-Ounce Jar Grape Leaves
1/2 Head Raw Cauliflower
2 Tablespoons Pine Nuts (Optional)
2 Tablespoons Raisins Or Currants (Optional)
1 Pound Ground Lamb
1/2 Medium Raw Onion
1 Tablespoon Dried Mint
1/2 Cup Fresh Parsley Leaves
2 Garlic Cloves
1 Teaspoon Salt
1/2 Teaspoon Ground Black Pepper
2 Fresh Lemons
1 Large Egg

Directions
1. Carefully remove the leaves from the jar and place in the sink or a large bowl. Cover with

hot water and allow to soak at least 15 minutes.
2. Break the cauliflower into small florets and remove the stems. Place them in the food processor bowl and let it pulse it all until it looks like rice.
3. Add raisins and pine nuts in a heated skillet, stirring often, letting it cook for about 3-5 minutes, until the nuts get slightly toasted. Leave it to cool, then finely chop, to get the full taste out of it. Add the nuts and raisins to the cauliflower rice in the bowl.
4. Place the lamb, salt and pepper, garlic, onion, mint, parsley in the bowl of a food processor and chop until the ingredients form a pâté and everything is combined. Add the lamb pâté to the rice and mix with your hands.
5. In a large saucepan, place a few small or torn leaves to cover the bottom of the pan. Drain the water from the rest of the leaves.
6. Take a leaf in your hand, spread it out, cut off the end and place about 1 tablespoon of filling on it. Roll it as tight as you can, then fold in the ends. Place the dolma rolls in the pan and gather them up close next to each other.

7. Place cut lemon slices on top of the dolmas in the pan. Press down on them with a heat-resistant plate, then add enough water to cover the plate for about an inch. Cover with a lid and let it boil. As soon as water is bubbling, let it simmer for 25-30 minutes, until the leaves are tender.
8. The plate will be hot. Carefully remove it and drain the pan of water. Let the dolmas stay covered afterwards so they stay warm.
9. Make a mix out of the remaining lemon juice and the egg, whisk it all until frothy and pour over the dolmas. Leave the lid on, as the heat will create a tasty coating over the dolmas.
10. Remove the dolmas from the pan and let them chill before you eat them.

Main Dish Recipes

Orange Grilled Chicken

Chicken is the favorite meat of the world and grilling, the designated method of cooking.

Ingredients

1 Lb. Chicken Breast - Boneless, Skinless
3 Cloves Garlic - Pressed
1 Tablespoon Herbes De Provence - Thyme, Oregano, Lavender
2 Tablespoons Agave Nectar Or Honey
1 Teaspoon Celtic Sea Salt
1 Tablespoon Chipotle Chile Powder
1 Cup Orange Juice - Freshly Squeezed

Directions

1. Wash chicken breasts and pat dry with a paper towel
2. Place the chicken in a 9 x 13 inch baking dish and pour the orange juice over it.
3. In a small bowl, combine Herbes de Provence, salt, garlic, chipotle and agave. Rub mixture onto chicken
4. Marinate chicken in the refrigerator for up to 5 hours
5. Grill each side of the chicken carefully
6. Bring the marinade to a boil, then reduce the heat and let it cook for 15 minutes longer.
7. Serve the chicken with marinade poured over it

Shepherd's Pie

This delicious meal has had centuries of variations, so here you have the Paleo version of this beloved pie.

Ingredients
2 Tablespoons Olive Oil
1 Large Onion - Diced
1 Pound Turkey or Pork Bacon, cut into 2 inch slices
2 Cups Diced Carrots
2 Cups Diced Celery
1 Pound Organic Grass Fed Ground Beef
1/2 Teaspoon Celtic Sea Salt
1 Teaspoon Ground Black Pepper
1/2 Teaspoon Smoked Paprika
1 Cup Chicken Broth
2 Large Heads Cauliflower - trimmed, chopped and steamed until very soft

Directions
1. Sauté onion in the olive oil for 15 minutes until soft
2. Add the bacon pieces and sauté until cooked – 10 minutes

3. Add celery and carrots and sauté in bacon fat until it softens – 10 minutes
4. Add beef and sauté until brown
5. Season with smoked paprika, pepper and salt
6. Cook together with the chicken broth until more than half of it has evaporated
7. Puree the cauliflower with olive oil until smooth
8. Pour the ground beef mixture into a medium sized (9" x 13") baking dish
9. Pour the cauliflower over beef
10. Bake at 350°F for 30 minutes

Thyme Salmon with Leek Coulis Sauce

In order for us to cook great salmon, we need to create this brilliant sauce, with a brilliant taste, which will fill your nose with the aroma of fresh herbs. Definitely worth a try.

Sauce Ingredients
1/2 Cup Olive Oil
2 Leeks, white part and two inches of green part
1 Fennel Bulb - finely chopped
1 Tablespoon Fresh Thyme - finely chopped
3 Cups Baby Spinach - roughly chopped
1 Cup Coconut Milk
1/4 Cup Lemon Juice - freshly squeezed
1/4 Teaspoon Celtic Sea Salt

Sauce Directions
1. Sauté leeks and fennel in the 1/4 cup olive oil for 6-8 minutes, to soften
2. Add thyme and spinach to skillet, cover for 2-3 minutes until the spinach wilts
3. Add coconut milk to mixture
4. Put the mixture in a blender and puree on high speed, until smooth

5. Add in lemon juice and salt
6. Add 1/4 cup olive oil
7. Pour over the salmon.

Thyme Salmon Ingredients
1 Pound Salmon
12 Sprigs Thyme
1 Tablespoon Olive Oil
1 Teaspoon Celtic Sea Salt

Salmon Directions
1. Heat oven to 500°F
2. Rinse salmon and pat dry
3. Place the thyme leaves on a parchment paper-lined baking sheet
4. Rub salmon with olive oil and sprinkle with salt, then place over the thyme
5. Turn off oven and place salmon in oven, baking for 10-12 minutes.

Asian Coconut Cauli-Rice Lettuce Wraps

Serving these wraps with pineapple will be as if opening the window on a perfect spring morning: everything fits. Remember: nothing ventured, nothing gained!

Ingredients

1/4 Cup Coconut Aminos, Paleo soy sauce
2 Tablespoons Fermented Fish Sauce
2 Tablespoons Lime Juice
1 Tablespoon Apple Cider Vinegar
1 Tablespoon Raw Honey
1 Egg
2 Tablespoons Coconut Oil
1 Medium Onion, Diced Small
1 Pound Ground Chicken
2 Tablespoons Grated Fresh Ginger
3 Cloves Garlic, Minced
1 Cup Packed Grated Carrot (2-3 carrots)
1 Large Red Bell Pepper - cut in small sticks
1/4 Small Head Green Cabbage
1 Head Butter Lettuce - leaves separated

Sea Salt and Pepper

Meat Mixture Directions

1. Whisk together the first 6 ingredients in a bowl, and set aside.
2. Melt coconut oil in a large skillet over medium heat.
3. Add onions and sauté for a few minutes until they are soft.
4. Add the chicken, break apart and cook it until the pink disappears.
5. Stir in the ginger, garlic and carrots. Cook for 3-5 minutes until the carrots soften.
6. Add red bell pepper and cabbage and stir for 3-5 minutes.
7. Pour the sauce mixture and toss the meat and vegetables to coat them evenly.
8. Reduce heat to low and simmer for another few minutes.
9. Place meat mixture on the lettuce leaves and top with coconut cauli-rice

Coconut Cauli-Rice Ingredients
1 Head Cauliflower
1/4-1/2 Cup Full Fat Coconut Milk

2-4 Tablespoons Coconut Oil
Salt and Pepper
3 Tablespoons Lime Juice

Coconut Cauli-Rice Directions

1. Take the cauliflower and cut it up into smaller pieces.
2. Place pieces in food processor and slowly pulse into a rice-like texture.
3. Sauté the cauliflower rice in skillet in the melted coconut oil for about 5 minutes until it becomes nice and soft.
4. Pour in the coconut milk and sauté for another 5 minutes.
5. Take off heat, add lime juice, salt and pepper.

Butternut Squash Harvest Lasagna

We all love Italian food, don't we? Their cuisine is among the most unique and tastiest around. It is only natural that the Paleo chefs have worked on adapting their food to the request of the public. And this is one of those glorious successes.

Ingredients
1 Pound Hot Italian Sausage - casing removed
1 Red Onion
3 Cloves Garlic
1 15 Ounce Can Pizza Sauce
1/2 Cup Roasted Red Peppers
1/4 Cup Extra Virgin Olive Oil
2 Leaves Fresh Basil
1 Small Butternut Squash
Cheese (Optional)

Directions
1. Heat over to 400ºF.

2. In a sauté pan, break the sausage into pieces while browning it. Add the garlic and the onions.
3. Cut off the top and ends of the squash and peel. Split it into quarters; right where the squash is bulbous, cut it in half, width-wise. Then cut in half lengthwise
4. Remove the seeds and slice the squash into the strips.
5. Puree the pizza sauce, olive oil, red peppers and basil in blender to make the sauce.
6. Pour a small amount of sauce in an oven safe dish, so it lightly covers its bottom. Add a single layer of squash, without overlapping the pieces.
7. Add the sausage mixture alternating with the sauce and squash. Repeat as many times as necessary, saving enough sauce to cover the top of the lasagna.
8. Bake for 45 minutes, until it forms a brown bubbly crust.
9. Let stand before cutting, to solidify.

Lemon Garlic Crockpot Chicken

When you're looking for a cooking challenge, you may be tempted to search for complicated recipes with weird ingredients. This one isn't complicated, the crockpot does all the work cooking the meat for 6 hours.

Ingredients
1 Whole Chicken
30-40 Cloves Of Garlic - peeled
1 Whole Lemon
1 White Onion - sliced
Salt And Pepper
<u>Homemade Italian Seasoning Blend:</u> equal parts of marjoram, thyme, rosemary, savory, sage, oregano, basil

Directions
1. Line the bottom of your pot or slow cooker with onions and garlic

2. Wash the chicken under cold water and pat dry
3. Put the chicken over the onions and garlic
4. Squeeze lemon juice all over the chicken
5. Season the inside and outside of your bird with plenty of salt, pepper and the Italian seasoning blend
6. Put lemon halves inside the chicken
7. Put the lid on the pot (or slow cooker) and let it cook on low for 6 hours, checking on it every now and again
8. Place the chicken on a plate, shred all the meat away from the bone.
9. Add meat to the broth, the garlic and onions.
10. Discard chicken carcass.
11. Serve to your hungry guests.

Poblano Chorizo Stuffed Peppers

In Romania, these are served on Christmas and Easter. You may substitute beef or chicken, but sausages are faster to cook and add a slightly spicy flavor.

Ingredients
5 Poblano Peppers
1/2 Pound Chorizo Sausage – brown, crumbled
1 Large Onion - thinly sliced and browned
1 Large Tomato - diced and browned

Directions
1. Preheat oven to 425°F.
2. Cut off tops of peppers, set aside. Remove seeds.
3. Combine onions, sausage and tomatoes.
4. Fill peppers and use the tops to cover them to help the peppers cook faster and retain their aroma.
5. Place the peppers on a lined baking sheet and bake for 20 minutes.

Sweet Potato Zucchini Frittata

Some recipes need to be fast when you're in a hurry. This is no exception. With inspiration from the Italians (again), is a meal that you can prepare when you are on the run, without sacrificing taste.

Ingredients
2 Tablespoons Ghee, Butter or Coconut Oil
8 Eggs
1 Large Sweet Potato - Peeled and Cut in Slices
2 Sliced Zucchinis
1 Sliced Red Bell Pepper
2 Tablespoons Fresh Parsley
  Salt and Pepper

Directions

1. Place potato slices in the oil in a hot skillet - 8 minutes
2. Add red bell pepper slices and the zucchini to potatoes. Cook - 4 minutes
3. Whisk the eggs, season with salt and pepper.
4. Add the eggs to the vegetables mixture in skillet

5. Cook on low heat until just set - 10 minutes
6. Keep the frittata under a heated broiler until it turns golden on top.
7. Cut into portions and garnish with parsley.
8. Delicious!

Honey Glazed Garlic Chicken Wings

The Game of Thrones fan within me is literally screaming at this recipe. All across the book, the meat of the nobles was always accurately detailed, important in the narrative and dripping of honey. There is this delicious image of steaming chicken, with sweet honey covering it in a crunchy crème-brûlée sort of way. It's mouth-watering and now it's readily available to be prepared in your household, with no Iron Throne to fret over. Try it and you'll understand.

Ingredients

3 Pounds Chicken Wings - separated
1/3 Cup Honey
1/4 Cup Water
2 Tablespoons Coconut Aminos
2 Tablespoons Apple Cider Vinegar
1/4 Cup Lemon Juice
2 Teaspoons Garlic Powder
3/4 Teaspoon Ground Ginger

1/4 Cup Sesame Seeds

Directions

1. Heat honey, water, aminos, vinegar, lemon juice, garlic and ginger in a small saucepan over medium-high heat.
2. Bring to boil, then turn heat down to low and let simmer for 5 minutes.
3. Set aside to cool.
4. Pour the honey marinade over chicken wings.
5. Place in the refrigerator for at least 2 hours.
6. Barbecue the chicken wings on grill, turning once – about 20 minutes.
7. Or place in a greased baking dish and bake at 400°F for 1 hour, turning once.
8. Sprinkle with sesame seeds. Garnish with hot red peppers if desired.

Zesty Roasted Leg of Lamb

The Greeks had this brilliant inspiration when it came to spicing up lamb and what they obtained is in a close tie with the Turkish version. An easy to make recipe, with plenty of variations to it.

Ingredients
4-5 Pound Leg of Lamb (boneless or bone in)
Zest of 2 Lemons
1/4 Cup Fresh Oregano - finely chopped, or use
3 Tablespoons dried oregano
5-6 Cloves Fresh Garlic - crushed
1 1/2 Teaspoons Salt
1/2 Teaspoon Cracked Pepper

Directions
1. Combine lemon zest, garlic, oregano, salt and pepper. Rub over the lamb roast.
2. Wrap it all in plastic wrap.
3. Place in refrigerator overnight or minimum of 4 hours.
4. Heat oven to 250°F.

5. Unwrap the roast and place the fat side down on a roasting pan.
6. Bake in oven for about 3 hours for rare, 3 ½ hours for medium-rare or about 4 hours for medium.
7. Broil roast for 5-7 minutes to give a crispy top.
8. Let rest, covered in foil for 10-20 minutes before slicing and serving.
9. Enjoy the feast!

Side Dish Recipes

From truly delicious rice to interesting variations on classic recipes, here you have everything you need to compliment the main dishes in this book. Ready?

Spicy Smashed Sweet Potatoes

Potatoes this time. And they're spicy, but they're sweet too. Enjoy this with a glass of red wine.

Ingredients
2 Medium Sized Sweet Potatoes

Spice Mixture Ingredients
1/2 Teaspoon Chili Powder
1/2 Teaspoon Cumin
1/2 Teaspoon Garlic Powder
1/2 Teaspoon Onion Powder
1/2 Teaspoon Paprika
1/2 Teaspoon Sea Salt
1/8 Teaspoon Ground Black Pepper

Sauce
1 Tablespoon Raw Honey
2 Tablespoons Olive Oil

Directions

1. Preheat the oven to 400°F.
2. While the oven is heating, mix together all ingredients for the spice mixture in a small bowl and set aside.
3. Poke small holes in the potatoes and place them all on the oven rack.
4. Cook for 40 minutes, so the potato gets cooked through.
5. Take the potatoes out of the oven, allow to cool.
6. Peel off skins.
7. Slice to about an inch and a half thickness.
8. Place on a cookie sheet, a few inches apart.
9. Gently press down on each sweet potato until the sides split open slightly, which will lead to their crispiness later on.
10. Mix the olive oil and the honey in a bowl and drizzle half the mixture over the sweet potatoes.
11. Take the spice mixture and sprinkle half of the mixture over each sweet potato.
12. Make sure it sticks by using a spatula or your hand and pressing it down.

13. Put the potatoes back in the oven and broil for 3-4 minutes, checking every now and then to make sure they don't burn.
14. Remove from oven and flip each potato over.
15. Drizzle the remaining sauce over the sweet potatoes, adding the remaining half of the spices.
16. Put back into the oven and broil for 3-4 minutes.
17. And you're done! Enjoy.

Fried Rice Cauliflower Style

I like rice and cauliflowers work great with anything. It's like bringing in Asia and Central Europe. Politics work and in this case, even the food does.

Ingredients
1 Head Of Cauliflower
4 Tablespoons Lard
4 Carrots - Peeled And Chopped
1 Small Onion - Chopped
2 Tablespoons Garlic - Chopped
1 Cup Green Peas
4 Eggs - Whisked
6 Tablespoons Coconut Aminos
1/2 Teaspoon Sesame Oil
1/2 Teaspoon Fish Sauce
Sea Salt And Ground Pepper To Taste

Directions

1. Whisk the eggs.
2. Place cauliflower in food processor and pulse until it resembles the size of rice.

3. Heat your skillet or wok over medium to high heat.
4. Add 2 Tablespoons of lard to the pan and let it melt.
5. Add the garlic, onions and carrots and cook for 3 minutes.
6. Add peas and cook for one more minute. Remove from pan and set aside.
7. In a separate pan, add your whisked eggs and scramble them, so they gain a slightly brown color. Add the salt and pepper
8. Place vegetables in a large bowl.
9. Add 2 Tablespoons of fat to the pan allow to melt.
10. Add the cauliflower rice to the pan coating with the oil. Cook for about 5-7 minutes, stirring every now and then until crispy.
11. Add the reserved vegetables back in the pan and stir well.
12. Next add the coconut aminos, sesame oil, fish sauce. Add pepper and salt to taste.
13. Serve and enjoy!

Orange and Ginger Glazed Carrots

For those of you loving carrots and vegetables next to your steaks, here you have the best of both worlds. Oranges are a great addition to any side dish, as they refresh and add flavor to any type of meal.

Ingredients
1 Pound Carrots - peeled and cut into 1/2" slices
1 Cup Water
Dash Sea Salt
1 Tablespoon Lard or Bacon Fat
1 Orange – save both the juice and zest
2 Tablespoons Raw Honey
1/2 Teaspoon Ground Ginger
Ground Black Pepper

Directions
1. Place the salt and the water in a saucepan.
2. Add the carrots and bring the water to a boil.
3. Next, reduce the heat and let simmer for 5 minutes until carrots are soft.

4. Drain the water.
5. Add the remaining ingredients (orange, honey and ginger) to the pan.
6. Stir to combine and sauté for 2-3 minutes
7. until carrots are very soft and the glaze is slightly thicker.
8. Add salt and pepper to taste.

Mexican Rice Cauliflower Inspired

Another recipe with cauliflower rice, but this time it's Mexican. Yes, this will be the spicy version. Make sure to have water close by while eating this.

Ingredients
1 Large Cauliflower, cut into florets
3 Tablespoons Bacon Fat
1 Small White Onion - chopped
3 Cloves Garlic, minced
1/2 Teaspoon Sea Salt
1/4 Teaspoon Ground Black Pepper
1/2 Teaspoon Cumin
1/2 Teaspoon Paprika
1/4 Cup Tomato Paste
1/4 Chopped Fresh Cilantro, more for garnish
1 Large Tomato, Chopped
2 Limes, Quartered (for serving garnish)

Directions
1. Grate the cauliflower florets in food

processor until they become as small as rice and set aside.
2. Heat the bacon fat in a large skillet over medium heat.
3. Add the chopped onion to the pan and sauté for 2 minutes.
4. Add the garlic and sauté for another minute.
5. Add the cauliflower to the pan and stir.
6. Add the black pepper, salt, paprika and cumin to the pan and stir to combine.
7. Allow mixture to cook for another 2-3 minutes, stirring occasionally.
8. Add the fresh cilantro, tomato paste and tomato. Stir until no liquid remains.
9. Cook for another 2-3 minutes, adding additional seasonings if desired.
10. Serve with tangy lime slices.

Sesame Noodles

No grains, remember? But these Paleo noodles are great. Just like Heaven on Earth.

Ingredients
1 Package Kelp Noodles
1/2 Tablespoon Coconut Oil
1/2 Tablespoon Minced Garlic
Dash Of Red Pepper Flakes (Optional)
1/4 Cup Almond Butter
1 Tablespoon Sesame Oil
1 Tablespoon Apple Cider Vinegar
1 Tablespoon Raw Honey
1 Tablespoon Coconut Aminos

Directions

1. Rinse the noodles and let them dry
2. Sauté the garlic for 2 minutes, in coconut oil at medium heat.
3. Add the vinegar, almond butter, honey, sesame oil and coconut aminos.
4. Stir until well combined.
5. Add the noodles to the pan and mix with the

sauce.
6. Sauté together for 3-5 minutes to get the noodles soft and sautéed through.
7. Serve!

Almond Yorkshire Pudding

A British mash-up this time. The Yorkshire Pudding is just like the Shepard's Pie, a century old recipe, this is our take on its Paleo version.

Ingredients
3 Eggs (room temperature)
1/2 Cup Almond Milk
1/2 Cup Arrowroot Powder
1/2 Teaspoon Sea Salt
3/8 Cup Beef Drippings

Directions

1. Whisk eggs, 1/8 cup beef drippings and almond milk together in a medium sized bowl.
2. Add the sea salt and the arrowroot powder to the mix and whisk it all together.
3. Let it set for an hour.
4. Heat oven to 400°F, placing a large square baking dish inside oven to heat.

5. Pour 1/4 cup beef drippings into the baking dish.
6. Heat drippings in the oven until they sizzle - 5 minutes.
7. Stir the egg mixture and quickly pour over the beef drippings.
8. Put back in the oven and bake for 30 minutes until the top becomes brown and puffy and the middle is cooked.
9. Remove from the oven and cut into slices.

Zucchini Noodles With Creamy Avocado

We're back to the zucchinis and noodles, so in case you've missed it, here we play again with the traditional ingredients to create something tastier and better.

Ingredients
5 Large Zucchinis -washed
1 Tablespoon Bacon Fat

Sauce
1 Large or 2 small Avocados – skin and pit removed
15 Fresh Basil Leaves
1 Teaspoon Sea Salt
1/2 Teaspoon Ground Pepper
3 Cloves Garlic - Crushed
2 Tablespoons Extra Virgin Olive Oil
1/2 Lemon - squeezed

Directions
1. Cut zucchini into long thin pieces resembling noodles.

2. Coat the zucchini with salt.
3. Place zucchini strips in a colander in the sink for 20 minutes to remove excess water.
4. Place all of the sauce ingredients in a food processor and blend it until smooth.
5. In a hot skillet, add the zucchini to the melted fat and cook for 2 minutes.
6. Add the sauce and toss to coat.
7. Cook for another 2-4 minutes.

Italian Breaded Eggplant

A mix between bread and simple eggplant, this breaded eggplant will truly test your taste, as all the spices will be truly felt. Are you ready for the challenge?

Ingredients
1 Medium Sized Eggplant (about 1 pound) - ends removed and thinly sliced
1 Large Egg
1/4 C. Arrowroot Powder
1/2 Teaspoon Sea Salt
1/4 Teaspoon Ground Black Pepper
1/4 Teaspoon Oregano
1/4 Teaspoon Thyme
1/4 Teaspoon Garlic Powder
Bacon Fat
Marinara Sauce (optional)

Directions
1. Place the eggplant in a colander and toss with sea salt.
2. Put colander in the sink for 20 minutes to remove the excess water.

3. Whisk the egg in a bowl. Set aside.
4. Place the arrowroot powder in second bowl and add the salt, pepper, thyme, garlic powder and oregano.
5. Stir to combine.
6. Wash the eggplant and pat dry.
7. Coat each eggplant slice first with egg mixture and then with arrowroot seasoning mixture.
8. Cover the bottom of a pan in bacon fat and heat on medium.
9. Fry the eggplant slices for 2 minutes on each side.
10. Let the eggplant drain on towels.
11. Arrange on a plate and serve with marinara sauce for dipping.

Sweet Potato Rolls

Yeah, here you have the ultimate bread-sort-of recipe. Basically, imagine macaroons without the sweetness, more like very crispy bread.

Ingredients
1 Sweet Potato – pierced with a fork
1/4 Cup Blanched Almond Flour
1 1/2 Cups Tapioca Flour
1 Teaspoon Baking Powder
1 Teaspoon Sea Salt
1/4 Cup Almond Milk
1/4 Cup Olive Oil
1 Large Egg
1/2 Cup Cooked Yams or Sweet Potatoes (about half of 1 small potato)
1 Tablespoon Ghee (Optional)

Directions
1. Heat oven to 400°F.
2. Place the sweet potato on a baking sheet lined with parchment paper and bake until tender - 30-35 minutes.

3. Cut open the top of the potato and let it cool.
4. Combine the almond flour with the tapioca flour, the baking powder and the sea salt in a bowl. Make sure they have no clumps. Set aside.
5. Combine the olive oil, almond milk, cooked potato and egg in a separate bowl. Mix on low speed, with a mixer, until well blended.
6. To this, slowly add half of the flour mixture from the first bowl. Mix the dough with your hands adding the remaining half the flour until gone. Knead for 2 minutes until it stops being sticky. Cover the dough with a kitchen towel and set aside for 10 minutes.
7. Roll the dough out into equal balls and place on a baking sheet covered with parchment paper, making sure there is enough space between each ball. Bake in the oven for 14-17 minutes and the tops get light brown.
8. Allow to cool for 15-20 minutes before serving.

Roasted Toasted Garlic Mushrooms

I'm a fan of mushrooms as a side dish and once you add the garlic, I'm done for. If you've never tried it, now's the time.

Ingredients
1 Pound Mushrooms
2-3 Tablespoons Olive Oil
1 Tablespoon Balsamic Vinegar
3-5 Cloves Garlic - minced or pressed
3 Pinches Dried Thyme
1-2 Pinches Cayenne Pepper
1/4 Teaspoon Salt - Or To Taste
1/4 Teaspoon Freshly Cracked Pepper
1-2 Tablespoons Fresh Parsley - chopped

Directions
1. Preheat oven to 400°F.
2. Wipe the mushroom clean.
3. Leave them whole and only cut them if they are large.

4. Combine the olive oil, balsamic vinegar, thyme, cayenne, garlic, salt and pepper in a bowl and mix.
5. Coat the mushrooms with this mixture.
6. Place mushrooms on a large baking sheet.
7. Roast in oven for 20-30 minutes.
8. Serve with fresh parsley

Soup Recipes

In this chapter you'll find interesting variations on classic recipes and perfect compliments to your main dishes.

Carrot Orange Ginger Soup

Would a "What's up, Doc?" be completely out of place here? Oh well, the rabbit is out of the hat already. If you needed an extra impulse to go back and watch Looney Tunes, you just got it.

Ingredients
2 Tablespoons Coconut Oil
1 Small Onion - peeled and chopped
5 Large Carrots - Chopped (around 1 pound)
1 Green Apple - Chopped
1/2 Ounce Fresh Ginger - chopped
1/3 Cup Orange Juice
1 Can Coconut Milk
2 Cups Chicken Stock
1/8 Teaspoon Cayenne Pepper (optional)
6 Drops Stevia to sweeten (optional)
Fresh Lime - for decoration

Directions
1. Sauté carrot, onion and apple in coconut oil until tender in saucepan
2. Add ginger, coconut milk, orange juice and stock to saucepan

3. Pour mixture into blender and puree, in small batches
4. Return mixture to saucepan and reheat until piping hot.
5. Stir in stevia and pepper.
6. Ladle into bowls and garnish with lime slices.
7. Serve with <u>Sesame Crisps Crackers</u>, <u>Herb Crackers</u> or <u>Paleo Rolls</u>, all recipes available in this book.

Chicken Stock From Scratch

This will be the basis of a hundred recipes all over the world of recipes. This stock will help you save time, maintaining the full range of flavors hidden within your typical chicken soup.

Ingredients

1 Chicken Carcass (bones left after cooking a full chicken and removing the meat)
3 Quarts Cold Water
1 Onion - halved
4 Carrots - cut into 2 inch pieces
10 Cloves Garlic – don't peel
1/4 Cup Parsley - finely chopped
10 Sprigs Fresh Thyme
5 Celery Tops (the leaves and ribs from the inside of a bunch of celery)
2 Bay Leaves
1 Tablespoon Apple Cider Vinegar

Directions

1. Put the chicken carcass in a large stockpot with the water
2. Boil and let it simmer
3. Set oven to 400°F, roast the carrots, onion and garlic cloves on a parchment lined baking sheet for one hour
4. Add the roasted vegetables to the chicken soup-wanna-be, then add celery, parsley, thyme, bay leaves and apple cider vinegar
5. Simmer the soup for one hour
6. Let it cool and put into glass jars to be used anytime a recipe calls for chicken stock

Mushroom Kale Chicken Soup

And here you shall come face to face with one of the numerous uses of chicken stock. Herbal-sort-of soups are the best, so enjoy the freshness of it.

Ingredients
2 Quarts Chicken Stock
1 Bunch Kale - chopped
3 Carrots - sliced
1 Cup Shiitake Mushrooms - sliced
1 Cup Shredded Chicken

Directions
1. Place the chicken stock in a pot over medium heat
2. Take two cups of stock along with the kale and blend in a blender
3. Pour this mix in the pot of soup stock
4. Add carrots, shredded chicken and the mushrooms
5. Cook for 30 minutes, add salt to taste
6. Enjoy the fresh taste of chicken soup made

from your own chicken stock!
7. Serve with <u>Sesame Crisps Crackers</u>, <u>Herb Crackers</u> or <u>Paleo Rolls</u>, all recipes available in this book.

Chicken Zucchini Noodle Soup

Using a Julienne slicer, here we have a noodle soup, with enough greens to be Paleo and enough meat to be delicious.

Ingredients
1 Quart Chicken Stock
1 Rib Celery - Diced
1 Large Carrot - Diced
1 Small Zucchini - made into noodles with julienne slicer or sharp knife

Directions
1. Bring chicken stock to a boil, then let it simmer
2. Add the carrots and the celery and simmer until tender - 10-20 minutes
3. Add the zucchini noodles and cook for 10 minutes
4. Serve with Sesame Crisps Crackers , Herb Crackers or Paleo Rolls, all recipes available in this book.

Salad Recipes

Because whatever it is, we love salads and we love them with anything. They cleanse the stomach, boost our energy and help with digestion.

Pomegranate Arugula Salad

If we are to interpret this salad's name by its original meaning, we are basically eating grenades. French humor, apparently.

Ingredients
4 Cups Arugula
1/2 Cup Pomegranate Seeds
3 Tablespoons Olive Oil
2 Tablespoons Balsamic Vinegar

Directions
1. Combine arugula and pomegranate seeds in a large bowl
2. Add olive oil and vinegar
3. Toss thoroughly
4. Enjoy!

Kale Grapefruit Salad

A strange mix? Nope, not this one. Grapefruit works brilliantly in salads, as it refreshes the taste better than vinegar alone.

Ingredients
1 Bunch Kale
1 Tablespoon Olive Oil
1/8 Teaspoon Celtic Sea Salt
1 Lime
1 Teaspoon Balsamic Vinegar
1 Grapefruit, Sliced And Chopped

Directions
1. Chop the kale thinly and add the olive oil.
2. Mix together with your hands.
3. Sprinkle Kale with lime juice, salt and vinegar.
4. Add the grapefruit and toss.
5. Let it sit for 15 minutes, to allow the flavors to saturate the kale.

Orange Cherry Mesclun Salad

In summer, this is the ultimate salad. You can't wish for anything better. Sweet, fresh and with the sun shining through it, this is one salad you'll love to dig into.

Ingredients
4 Cups Mesclun Greens or other Mixed Spring Greens
3 Oranges - sliced into triangle wedges
1 Cup Cherries - pitted and cut in half
2 Tablespoons Olive Oil
2 Tablespoons Balsamic Vinegar

Directions
1. Place oranges, cherries and greens in a salad bowl.
2. Drizzle with olive oil and vinegar.
3. Toss with greens and enjoy.

Dessert Recipes

It's dessert. You can't just skip it. It's an essential part of our society. Ready for some real eye-candy?

Banoffee Cashew Cheesecake

And yes, finally we get to the ultimate desert: cheesecake. And not just any cake, but the universally acknowledged best cake of history.

Ingredients

Crust Layer
1 Cup Almond Flour
3 Tablespoons Ghee
1/8 Cup Raw Honey - warmed
1 Teaspoon Vanilla Extract
1/4 Teaspoon Sea Salt

Banana Cheesecake Layer
2 Cups Raw Cashews - Soaked In Water Overnight (or boil for 20 minutes)
1/2 Cup Ghee
2 Medium Sized Ripe Bananas
2 Tablespoons Lemon Juice
1/4 Cup Raw Honey

Toffee Layer
1 Can (13/14 Oz.) Full Fat Coconut Milk
1/4 Cup Raw Honey

2 Tablespoons Ghee
1/2 Teaspoon Vanilla Extract
Dash Sea Salt

Whipped Coconut Cream Layer
1 Can (13/14 Oz.) Full Fat Coconut Milk – place in refrigerator for 6 hours or more
1/4 Cup Raw Honey
1/2 Teaspoon Vanilla Extract

Topping
1 Ripe Banana, Sliced
Dash Cacao Powder

Directions

Crust Layer
1. Preheat the oven to 350°F.
2. Mix the crust ingredients until well combined.
3. Place in the oven on a parchment-lined baking sheet, make sure it is an even layer and bake for 15 minutes. Let it cool.

Banana cheesecake layer

1. Add all of Banana Cheesecake layer the ingredients into a blender and mix until smooth - 2 minutes. Scrape the edges for a better mix of ingredients.
2. Pour the cheesecake layer on top of the crust layer and place in the freezer.

Toffee layer

1. Place all of the Toffee layer ingredients in a medium sized saucepan over medium heat. Let it boil for about 30-40 minutes, stirring occasionally.
2. It will start to darken, so stir continually to keep it from burning. Once the mixture is thick and amber colored, pour over the banana cheesecake layer.
3. Return the pan to the freezer and let it set for about 1 hour.

Whipped coconut cream layer

1. Scrape the coconut cream from the can and place in a bowl. Add the honey and vanilla ingredients and whip together until puffy.
2. Place the cream on top of the previous layer.

Assembling

1. Add the sliced bananas and a sprinkle of the cacao powder to the top of the cheesecake.

Apple Pie Parfaits

Yes, we can do this. It's a recipe with several steps, but not as hard as it looks.

Ingredients
Apple Pie Filling
5 Large Apples (your favorite variety) - peeled, cored and sliced
1/3 Cup Ghee
1/3 Cup Raw Honey
1/2 Teaspoon Ground Cinnamon
1 Teaspoon Vanilla Extract
1 Teaspoon Arrowroot Powder
Dash Sea Salt

Crumb Topping Ingredients
3/4 Cup Blanched Almond Flour
3 Tablespoons Raw Honey
3 Tablespoons Ghee or Soft Butter
1/2 Teaspoon Ground Cinnamon
Dash Sea Salt

Whipped Coconut Cream Ingredients (optional)

1 Can Full Fat Coconut Milk - refrigerate for 6 or more hours
1 Tablespoon Vanilla Extract
2 Tablespoons Raw Honey

Apple Pie Filling Directions

1. Combine the honey, ghee, cinnamon, vanilla extract, salt and arrowroot powder in a saucepan.
2. Place over medium heat and bring to a boil, stirring often.
3. Add the apples and reduce the heat to low.
4. Let it simmer for 10 minutes, so the apples get tender. Stir to coat them in sauce.
5. Remove from heat and allow to cool.

Crumb Topping Directions

1. Place all ingredients in a medium sized mixing bowl and stir with a fork until crumbly. Set aside.

Whipped Coconut Cream Directions

1. Keep the coconut milk in the fridge for 6 or more hours, to separate the cream
2. Scrape out the cream into a bowl.

3. Add the honey and the vanilla to the mixture. Whip the cream with a mixer until well blended.

Assembling
1. Place the cool apple pie filling in a single serving bowl.
2. Top with crumb topping and then a scoop of the whipped coconut cream.
3. Sprinkle with some cinnamon
4. Serve to friends and family who will be so impressed!

Strawberry Leather

Imagine eating long strips of fruity leathers. Weird sounding, I know, but so tasty! It's not just for kids anymore.

Ingredients
4 Cups Strawberries or Any Other Soft Fruit You Want

Directions
1. Preheat oven to 150°F. Line a cookie sheet with parchment paper.
2. Wash your fruit, allow to dry
3. Cut fruit into small pieces
4. In a blender, puree the fruit until smooth.
5. Pour the pureed fruit onto the pan, spreading it out evenly. Bake for eight hours or as long as needed to become leathery.

Coconut Butter Stuffed Dates

Like French Macaroons with a twist!

Ingredients
10 Pitted Dates
1 Cup Coconut Butter - Melted

Directions
1. Slice open each date, without cutting all the way through
2. Stuff each date with melted coconut butter, as much as you can fit in, making sure you can still close it.
3. Allow coconut butter to cool. Enjoy this sweet Paleo treat!

Fruit Dip

It's a fruit dip. It's the more elegant version to tortillas and tomato sauce and it won't show on your hips.

Ingredients
1 Cup Coconut Milk
1 Teaspoon Vanilla Extract
2 Ripe Bananas
2 Teaspoons Coconut Flour
1 1/2 Tablespoons Unsweetened Cocoa Powder (optional)

Directions
1. Place all the ingredients into a blender, except for the cocoa powder
2. Blend until creamy
3. Add the cocoa. Process again until the dip is well mixed.
4. Allow it to thicken in the refrigerator.
5. Serve with fresh fruit for a refreshing snack.

Snack Recipes

If you're feeling munchy and want something without losing all that weeks' worth of healthy Paleo eating, here you have the healthier alternatives.

Coconut Chicken Nuggets BBQ Sauce

Another tasty football night treat is a twist on the classic KFC chicken and sauce. While retaining the taste, this one adds coconut to the mix. Stand back for the rave reviews!

Ingredients
1 Pound Ground Chicken
1 Egg Yolk
1 Teaspoon Onion Powder
1/4 Teaspoon Garlic Powder
1/4 Teaspoon Paprika
1/4 Teaspoon Sea Salt
1/4 Teaspoon Fresh Ground Black Pepper
1/2 Cup + 1/3 Cup Almond Flour
1/2 Cup Unsweetened Shredded Coconut
1/2 Cup Coconut Oil
Salt & Pepper

Directions
1. Preheat oven to 375°F.
2. In a bowl combine 1/2 cup coconut, 1/4 cup almond flour and salt & pepper.
3. In a separate bowl, combine 1/3 cup almond flour, the ground chicken, onion powder, garlic powder, pepper, sea salt, egg yolk and

paprika.
4. Mix well.
5. Roll 2 Tablespoons of the chicken mixture into a ball.
6. Dip it in the coconut and almond bowl mixture.
7. Repeat until all chicken mixture is used.
8. Place the nuggets into the heated coconut oil in skillet. In small portions, fry each side for 3 to 4 minutes.
9. Cover baking pan with parchment paper.
10. Move the nuggets to baking pan.
11. Allow to cook in the oven for 4 to 5 minutes.
12. Let the nuggets to cool and serve with the Paleo BBQ sauce below.

Paleo "BBQ" Sauce

Ingredients
1 Tablespoon Coconut Oil
4 Tablespoons Shallots - minced
4 Cloves Garlic - minced
3/4 Cup Fresh Orange Juice
2 Tablespoons Apple Cider Vinegar
10 Tablespoons Tomato Paste

1/2 Teaspoon Mustard Powder
1/2 Teaspoon Paprika
1/2 Teaspoon Salt
1/4 Teaspoon Pepper

Directions

1. Pour coconut oil into saucepan. Heat on medium.
2. Add garlic and shallots to pan and cook until soft.
3. Stir in remaining ingredients and simmer over low heat for 15-20 minutes.
4. Serve with nuggets on the side.

Egg Muffins

Best thing for breakfast or the midnight breakfast (maybe at Tiffany's)...

Ingredients

6 Eggs
1 Cup Salami - diced
2/3 Cup Halloumi Cheese – diced (optional)
1 Medium White Onion - peeled and diced
Sea Salt
Cracked Pepper
2 Tablespoons Olive Oil

Directions

1. Sauté onion in olive oil until golden. Set aside.
2. Fry the cheese on both sides, to gain a golden crust. Add the sautéed onion.
3. Add the salami to this mix.
4. Heat the oven to 170°C.
5. Whisk the eggs.
6. Spray the baking muffin molds with olive oil.
7. Divide the salami and cheese filling into the bottoms of the muffin molds.

8. Pour in whisked eggs on top of salami mixture.
9. Stir gently to combine the ingredients
10. Bake for 20-25 minutes, on the middle shelf of the oven.

Chicken-And-Egg-Stuffed Tomatoes

A really fast and simple dish, it even work as a quick breakfast

Ingredients
Chicken – cooked and diced fine
1 Egg – hardboiled and peeled
Vinaigrette of your choice (several are found in this cookbook)
Ripe Tomatoes

Directions
1. Mash hardboiled egg.
2. Add finely diced chicken to egg mixture.
3. Add vinaigrette to egg chicken mixture and stir thoroughly.
4. Cut top off tomato and hollow out.
5. Fill hollowed-out tomatoes with egg chicken mixture for a healthy treat.

Guacamole Eggs

Some like it hot! Or how to burn your insides with every bite.

Ingredients
4 Eggs - hard-boiled and peeled
1 Avocado
2 Teaspoons Hot Sauce
1 Teaspoon Lemon Juice
Sea Salt (optional)
Freshly Ground Black Pepper

Directions
1. Take eggs and cut in half lengthwise.
2. Remove yolks and serve the white part of the egg
3. Peel, pit and mash avocado.
4. Mash egg yolks
5. Mix yolks and avocado with hot sauce and lemon juice.
6. Season with salt and pepper to taste.
7. Refill egg whites with the egg yolk mixture.
8. Serve with plenty of water nearby!

Lime Chicken Wings

Chicken wings for everybody. We should do a sitcom all revolving around everyone's love for chicken. And chicken wings.

Ingredients
1/2 Medium Onion - roughly chopped
2 Jalapeno Peppers (or 1 serrano pepper) - ribs and seeds removed
3 Garlic Cloves, peeled
1/2 Cup Cilantro - tightly packed
Freshly Ground Pepper
Zest from 2 Limes
1/4 Cup Lime Juice
2 Tablespoons Fish Sauce
2 Tablespoons Coconut Aminos
6 Pounds Chicken Wings and/or Drumsticks
1-2 Tablespoons Coconut Oil
4 Limes - Cut Into Wedges

Directions
1. Toss the onion, garlic, peppers, ground pepper, cilantro, lime zest and juice, coconut aminos and fish sauce into a blender

2. Blend to a puree consistency to create marinade.
3. Place the chicken wings in a large bowl and pour the marinade on top.
4. Mixing it all together with your hands, to make it easier.
5. Marinate the chicken in the refrigerator for at least 30 minutes or longer (but no more than 10 hours).
6. Let the wings warm to room temperature before you intend to cook them.
7. Heat oven to 425°F.
8. Line a rimmed baking sheet with foil, place a greased wire grilling rack on foil.
9. Arrange the wings on the wire rack.
10. Roast for 30 minutes and flip the wings halfway through.
11. Serve with lime wedges to your raving fans.

Yummy Fish Sticks

Kids love them but tasty and healthy enough for the whole family to love.

Ingredients
1 Pound White Fish (Cod, Snapper or Tilapia)
2 Eggs - whisked
1 Cup Blanched Almond Flour
1 Teaspoon Celtic Sea Salt
1/4 Cup Olive Oil
1/4 Cup Grape seed Oil

Directions
1. Wash fish fillets in cold water, dry with paper towels and set on a plate
2. Cut the fish into pieces and remove any bones
3. Place whisked eggs in a shallow dish.
4. Place flour with salt in a separate shallow dish.
5. Coat the fish sticks first with the egg, then coat by rolling in the flour
6. Heat 2 tablespoons grape seed oil and 2 Tablespoons olive oil in a skillet and cook

the fish sticks for 4 minutes on each side, or until browned.
7. Move the fish sticks to a paper towel covered plate to absorb any extra oil
8. Repeat until all fish pieces are cooked. Use fresh oil for every new batch of fish sticks.
9. Serve with tomato juice

Fruit Nutty Energy Bars

Quick, simple and useful. Energy in a handful. No more grains, only fruits and nuts. Have fun making them.

Ingredients

1 Cup Nuts of your choice
1 Cup Dried Fruit of your choice
1 Cup (12-15 Whole) Pitted Dates

Directions

1. Roast the nuts at 350°F for 10-12 minutes. Let them cool.
2. Combine nuts, dried fruit and date in food processor. Process it all for 30 so seconds, to get it all crumbled. Separate the dates if they start to clump together.
3. Process continuously for 2 minutes, until a ball is formed.
4. Cover your work surface in plastic wrap and place the dough on it.
5. Wrap the dough in plastic wrap. Press and knead until it forms a thick dough square.
6. Wrap and let it chill overnight (or a minimum of an hour if you're in a hurry).

7. Unwrap the chilled dough and cut into 8 large bars or 16 smaller bars. Wrap each bar separately in waxed paper or plastic wrap.
8. Store the bars in a cool place to keep out the heat to maintain their firmness.
9. Remember to pack one in your gym bag for a refreshing snack after your workout.

Blueberry Balls

Something sweet out of nowhere. It should be a dessert, but we're calling it a snack.

Ingredients
Slivered Almonds
Dehydrated Apple Chunks
1/4 Cup Dried Blueberries
1/4 Cup Almond Butter (or other nut butter)
1/4 Cup Raw Honey
1 Teaspoon Cinnamon
Pinch Of Salt

Directions
1. Mix all ingredients together in bowl.
2. Take a teaspoon full amount of dough in your hand and shape into balls.
3. Place balls in covered container not allowing them to touch.
4. Refrigerate for half an hour to set.
5. A delicious healthy treat anytime.

Prosciutto Chips

Yes, bacon without all the fat! This is so crispy you will never ever feel like eating anything else.

Ingredients
3 Ounces Of Thinly Sliced Prosciutto Di Parma – Make sure they are paper thin and as fresh as possible

Directions
1. Preheat the oven to 350°F with the oven rack in the middle.
2. Cover a baking sheet in parchment paper and place the prosciutto on top, making sure not to overcrowd it and keeping the pieces apart.
3. Bake for 10-15 minutes, until they're all crunchy, but keep an eye on them, as they can get burned very fast.
4. Let the chips cool. They'll get crunchier as they cool.

Herb Crackers

The sesame crackers with a twist, this is like a French perfume ready to explode in your mouth. The best part of cooking with herbs is that it fills your kitchen with a fresh aroma, which will stay for days after you finish eating the crackers.

Ingredients
2 Cups Almond Flour
1/2 Teaspoon Sea Salt
2 Tablespoons Your Favorite Herbs Of Choice, with Rosemary
2 Tablespoons Water
1 Egg White
1 Tablespoon Olive Oil
1/4 Teaspoon Coconut Oil

Directions
1. Preheat oven to 350°F.
2. Combine salt, almond flour and herbs in a medium bowl.

3. Combine the egg white, olive oil, water, and melted coconut oil. Whisk ingredients together.
4. Add the wet ingredients to the flour ingredients in first bowl and stir until a dough forms.
5. Add water or oil only if it doesn't stick together as a dough ball.
6. Place dough between two sheets of parchment paper. Roll out to an even thickness of 1/4 inch thick.
7. Transfer parchment to a baking sheet pan and remove the top parchment. Trim the edges and cut the dough into crackers.
8. Bake for 10 minutes, let them set in the oven for 10 minutes with the heat turned off.
9. Goes well with Hummus recipe found earlier in this cookbook.

Thank You!

If you've enjoyed this PaleoRecipe Book, would you please take a minute to leave a review on Amazon? Even just a few sentences would be great.

When you leave a review it helps others who are looking for healthy Paleo recipes that are Gluten Free, Wheat Free, Sugar Free and Dairy Free to help them **Lose The Wheat And Lose The Weight**.

Be sure to download your FREE printable meal plans and shopping lists here: http://PaleoRecipesWeightLoss.com/bonus

Thank you,

Beth Gabriel

Book Recommendations

- 50 Paleo Amazing BBQ Recipes - http://www.amazon.com/dp/B00KQ285PY

- 50 Clean Eating Paleo Diet, Gluten Free Recipes - http://www.amazon.com/dp/B00NRRK0FI

- Against The Grain – http://www.amazon.com/dp/1936608367

- Paleo For Beginners - http://www.amazon.com/ /dp/1623150310

- Paleo Slow Cooker - http://www.amazon.com/dp/1499621914

ALL RIGHTS RESERVED. No part of this publication may be reproduced or transmitted in any form whatsoever, electronic, or mechanical, including photocopying, recording, or by any informational storage or retrieval system without express written, dated and signed permission from the author.

DISCLAIMER AND/OR LEGAL NOTICES:
Every effort has been made to accurately represent this book and it's potential. Results vary with every individual, and your results may or may not be different from those depicted. No promises, guarantees or warranties, whether stated or implied, have been made that you will produce any specific result from this book. Your efforts are individual and unique, and may vary from those shown. Your success depends on your efforts, background and motivation.

The material in this publication is provided for educational and informational purposes only and is not intended as medical advice. The information contained in this book should not be used to diagnose or treat any illness, metabolic disorder, disease or health problem. Always consult your physician or health care provider before beginning any nutrition or exercise program. Use of the programs, advice, and information contained in this book is at the sole choice and risk of the reader.